Meet the BEATLES

written and
compiled by **TONY BARROW**

with an introduction by the Beatles themselves

Souvenir Press

CONTENTS

Personal Portraits Beatle Background

Beatling Beside the Seaside

Back Home with the Beatles

Chart-toppers at their Moment of Truth

Stars of Stage, Home-Screen & Radio

A London Day in the Life of the Beatles

Acknowledgements

The author and publishers wish to acknowledge with thanks the kind co-operation of Dezo Hoffmann, Peter Kaye, Graham Spencer, Stan McLeod, Cyrus Andrews, A.B.C. Television

First published in Great Britain in 1963 by Souvenir Press Ltd
43 Great Russell Street, London WC1B 3PD

This collector's edition published in 2014

The right of Tony Barrow to be identified as the author of this work has been asserted in accordance with section 77 of the Copyright, Designs and Patents Act, 1988

ISBN 9780285642898

Printed and bound in Croatia under the supervision of MRM Graphics Ltd

From Us to You

a personal introduction to "meet the beatles" by

GEORGE, JOHN, PAUL and RINGO

WE look upon this book as a very welcome way of meeting a lot of new and old friends all over the country. We try to see as many Beatle People as we can when we're out on tour but we can't hope to fit in too many chats with backstage visitors because we just can't find the time to do so. Guess we spend something like twenty-six hours a day working, travelling and eating—which seems to leave something like minus two hours for a spot of kip! However, gagging apart, we want to express our appreciation to everyone concerned in the production of "Meet The Beatles". The pages which follow have been crammed with pictures and stories which more or less trace out the landmarks of our combined and individual histories from before the days of "Love Me Do" up to the present time.

One of the questions people ask us is that old columnist's chestnut "How has stardom changed you?" The simple answer is that it HASN'T!

We stay in lots of towns and cities we wouldn't have managed to visit if our records hadn't done so well. We have a wide new circle of show-biz friends we'd never even spoken to before the beginning of 1963. It gives us a pretty fab feeling to see each of our record releases climbing through the Top Twenty. We feel great when concert audiences give us a terrific reception and we've got a lot more money to spend on clothes and musical equipment these days.

But these things don't change us as people. The life may be lived faster but the personality doesn't alter. We preserve one single outlook upon our professional lives—to do as well as we can wherever and whenever we're performing whether we've got an audience of a hundred or ten thousand.

We're just as nutty, just as happy and just as handsome (*Ringo wrote that last bit so we won't give him his sticks until he rubs it out*) as we've always been.

It is the people around us who have changed. They've been caught up in some kind of whirlwind which doesn't seem to blow more than a breeze around us Beatles ourselves. They move about much more briskly and say lots of important things. They bring us exciting news about sales figures, chart positions and silver disc awards. They tell us we're due at a ballroom three hundred miles away by this evening so we'd better hurry up and finish our breakfasts. They worry for us if new stage uniforms don't come through on schedule or if someone has mislaid a set of airline tickets which we'll be needing tomorrow.

In the middle of all this hectic activity and busy bustle we just sit and sign lots of autographs until it's time for us to go out on stage and sing or play just the way we've been singing and playing for the last three years around Merseyside. If ever we did begin to feel overwhelmed by the fab things which have been happening we'd all get nasty big heads. Luckily there are three other Beatles ready to sit on any one of us who may show signs of swelling about the bonce, so we don't think it will happen!

What we're really trying to say is that we owe an awful lot to the folk who work around us and keep everything organized on our behalf. They're the ones who do all the extra dashing around and all the extra jobs.

The pop scene is crowded with very wonderful people. That's what makes our new lives in the centre of the entertainment world so enjoyable. So far as we're concerned as a group, we are surrounded by people who just couldn't be more helpful and more understanding. First there's our manager, Brian Epstein of Nems Enterprises, who was responsible for bringing us to the attention of the record company and for helping us to get our first crack at the Top Twenty charts. Second there's our recording manager, George Martin, who supervises and produces our studio sessions for the Parlophone label. George has a terrific sense of humour (he ought to have since he has worked with brilliant comics like Peter Sellers and Spike Milligan) and a matching amount of patience. Third there's Dick James, the music publisher, who seems to be able to tell us exactly when our last disc was at No. 12 in Israel and how quickly he thinks our next one will be in Australia's Top Ten.

Last, and by no means least, there is Neil Aspinall, who is the group's road manager. He's the guy who has to make sure we've got the right plugs on our amplifiers and that we haven't got more than a hundred or so fans in our dressing room at any one time. Neil has a new assistant now (his name is Malcolm Evans) to drive our van.

We'd like to close this introduction by letting you know how much we value every burst of applause, every fan letter, every hit record. These are the things which tell us YOU like what we're doing and this, in our opinion, is all that really matters.

Thanks a million all you Beatle People——
——you're the gear!

John Lennon   Paul McCartney   George Harrison   Ringo Starr

lead guitar beatle . . .

George Harrison

GEORGE HARRISON is the youngest member of The Beatles. He went to the same primary school as John Lennon and the same high school as Paul McCartney.

His intense interest in all things musical dates back to his early teens although he had his schoolboy mind set on a career which would be based upon his equally powerful flair for painting and drawing. Even in primary school days he shared this flair with a youthful John Lennon who was also at Dovedale Road. Because of the difference in their ages John and George didn't become friendly until after their scholastic paths parted at eleven-plus level.

George's art master suggested there was a more-than-fair chance of his creative talent developing to such an extent that he might become a famous painter in later life.

George recalls: "While most of the other lads spent their Wednesday afternoons panting round the school running track I would be content to take a notebook and dream up some new sketches—most of them from somewhere inside my head and not from the lively scene around me. I was fond of sport—specially swimming and athletics—in the early years but I was fonder still of art. I could never settle to routine things like mugging up historical dates and working out the solutions to mathematical formulae. They left me cold because they didn't offer any sort of challenge. You just learnt off loads of facts and figures. I wanted to make something new instead of following the example of other people. I enjoyed anything which allowed me plenty of freedom of expression and personal control over design and method. I suppose this led me towards making my own music without being taught to play or sing. I could find scope with a guitar which I couldn't find with a theorem or a grammar book".

Although that worthy academy of learning did not know it at the time, Liverpool Institute High School had a wealth of latent pop talent in its midst. At the end of term when students were given a free hand to fill in their post-examination hours George and Paul would get together to try out their first home-made amplifiers and second-hand guitars in an empty lecture room. Next door Les Chadwick (bass guitarist with Gerry's popular Pacemakers) was busily building up instrumental excitement in another classroom with pals who have since found important positions within the ranks of other Beat City recording groups.

When George left school he went in for electrical engineering and took up his trade as an apprentice with the perfectionist approach which eventually made his presence amongst the Beatle foursome so invaluable.

George's personality mixes a deeply ingrained desire to be artistically ingenious with a personal pride which causes him to tackle any task with maximum enthusiasm providing he has faith in its successful outcome. He has an unusual capacity for thought and an excellent memory for faces, places and names. By nature he is kind, fairly quiet, invariably helpful, noticeably considerate of other folk's feelings, swift to sum up the character of those whom he is introduced to and loath to end any friendship of long or short standing.

Although he is less evident in the group's vocal spotlight than colleagues Paul or John, he proves himself to be an excellent singer with a particularly engaging style of delivery when it comes to balladeering. Instrumentally, it is George's intricately fingered lead guitar which drives out the forceful backing themes to every Beatle performance.

With The Beatles, George finds ample outlet for his creative abilities and he must be one of the most contented professional musicians on the British pop scene today.

GEORGE'S BEATLETISTICS: Born in Liverpool, 25 February 1943. Measures 5 ft. 11 in., weighs 10 st. 2 lb. Eyes: hazel. Hair: dark brown. Founder member of the group in 1960. Favours smallish blondes, driving, sleeping, watching television, the singing of Eartha Kitt and the guitar playing of Chet Atkins and Segovia. Hates haircuts. Has two brothers and one sister.

rhythm guitar beatle . . .

John Lennon

JOHN LENNON is the most "way out" member of The Beatles so far as his ideas of humour and his general approach to life are concerned. Yet his natural tendency towards the off-beat and the unusual is tempered by a degree of sound business sense which balances up his personality and serves The Beatles well when routine professional problems look as though they might grow into awkward situations without his thorough counsel.

At Liverpool's Dovedale Road Primary School he knew a three-years-younger George Harrison by sight. When the two went to different grammar schools their teenage careers followed remarkably similar lines. At Quarrybank John concentrated on art and took a great dislike to subjects like science. He was keen on swimming but spent a great deal of time writing satirical poetry. Composing original songs and poems, creating symbolic artwork and developing a goon-type zeal for comic comment on life as he has found it, fill major portions of his existence.

John's assorted recollections of school life go like this: "I gather I used to embarrass authority by chanting out a weird version of "The Happy Wanderer" at inappropriate moments. I was suspended for a spell. Think it was either for eating chocolate in prayers or ducking a swimming instructor. Something daft like that. George was a great buddy even by that time. He came over to Quarrybank one day to sign on as a candidate for the G.C.E. art paper ... although he was suppose to be taking it at Liverpool Institute! We did an thing for laughs. When I left Quarrybank I went Liverpool College of Art with an idea that I mig finish up drawing gorgeous girls for toothpas posters. In the holidays I went over to Hanover make some money as a temporary labourer building sites. I spent most of my wages having good time in Germany but there was enough left pay for my first electric guitar. The poetry bit? still churn out odd verses whenever somethi strikes me as being particularly funny or rea ludicrous. Expect they'll go into book-form sor day when I collect all the cigarette packets together

The Lennon make-up is essentially one constantly changing ideals, although it sticks o a mile that he'll always devote a good slice of time and energy to collaborating with Paul on son writing activities. Like the rest of the quartet, Jo is a self-taught singer and instrumentalist yet he brilliant at on-the-spot modifications to music arrangements. His leather-coated voice can whip tremendous strength and he's in his vocal eleme when he's working on a real ravin' rocker li "Twist And Shout".

John has forthright opinions on everything whic concerns him directly or indirectly. He has t courage of his convictions and will leap into t most heated argument if he feels strongly about a subject under discussion.

JOHN'S BEATLETISTICS: Born in Liverpool, 9 October 1940. Measures 5 ft. 11 in., weighs 11 st. 5 lb. Eyes: brow Hair: brown. Founder member of the group in 1960. Puts immense feeling into his performances—which include harmoni phrases and falsetto voice effects. Enjoys listening to modern jazz, adores jelly and cornflakes, makes a bee-line for blond who are intelligent and for records by The Shirelles. Dislikes traditional jazz and thick heads. Has two stepsisters.

bass guitar beatle . . .

Paul McCartney

PAUL McCARTNEY was the brainy Beatle at school. At Liverpool Institute he took his G.C.E. and came out with five passes—which persuaded his masters and his father that Paul should think about going on for university entrance. He stayed at school for a two-year sixth form course and was successful in English Literature at advanced level.

Paul has plenty of school-day memories: "Less than a year separated George and I so far as age is concerned. We shared a dislike of subjects such as geography and mathematics. We were both fond of swimming at one stage and I remember betting him ten bob (big stakes at the time!) that he couldn't swim the Mersey from the Liverpool Pier Head to Birkenhead. Neither of us attempted it in the end because it was rather cold and we didn't like the look of the oily water down by the docks. But we did take each other on at other bets—like going off on a hitch-hiking holiday and seeing who would have to spend any money first. We went for twenty-eight hours without food before buying a tin of spaghetti to cook on a primus stove—and we slept on a beach at Taunton and a football pitch in Wales. The only time I won bets with George was when I challenged him to write sentences backwards. I found I had the knack of doing that. Maybe because I've always been left-handed. When I began to teach George how to play the guitar he got very mixed up because I was working with my left hand. Eventually I got him to play his first chord—G 7— and we celebrated so loudly in the school library that someone came in to give us 500 lines!"

Around the time Paul left school in the summ of 1960 The Beatles were on the point of formi themselves into a semi-pro outfit. At some u chronicled stage of that year Paul and John s themselves up as a temporary duo act—The Nu Twins—just for laughs. Otherwise, Paul move straight from the classroom to local club and dan hall stages as a founder member of The Beatles.

When The Beatles went to Germany, Paul knowledge of three languages came in very hand His expert handling of the guitar, his finely d veloped sense of humour and his eagerness participate in the group's vocal performances can in equally handy!

Paul's personality is uncomplicated. He laps life, has a ball when he's singing to a "live" audien and has no fear of the hard work which any succes ful entertainers have to put in on rehearsal. Wi almost uncanny regularity he finds it possible turn out hit songs in collaboration with composi colleague John. Of the tunesmith side of thin, Paul says: "Sometimes a catchy phrase comes fir and sometimes one of us puts forward a promisi title-line to start off the lyrics. Either way we ha occasionally written a completely new number less than an hour. Usually it takes longer these day We get snatches of an idea and have to postpo work on it because we're travelling so much. Wha ever happens I never want to give up writing an I'm pretty sure John and I will stick together on th because we seem to have a combination of ide which turn themselves into pop hits".

PAUL'S BEATLETISTICS: Born in Liverpool, 18 June 1942. Measures 5 ft. 11 in., weighs 11 st. 4 lb. Eyes: brown. Hai very dark brown. Founder member of the group in 1960. Has a strong liking for Kraft cheese slices, all types of we performed music except traditional jazz, long-haired girls who are witty conversationalists, films which star Sophia Lor or Natalie Wood, records made by Little Richard or Dinah Washington and doodling about on Ringo's drum kit. Hat having to shave. Has one brother.

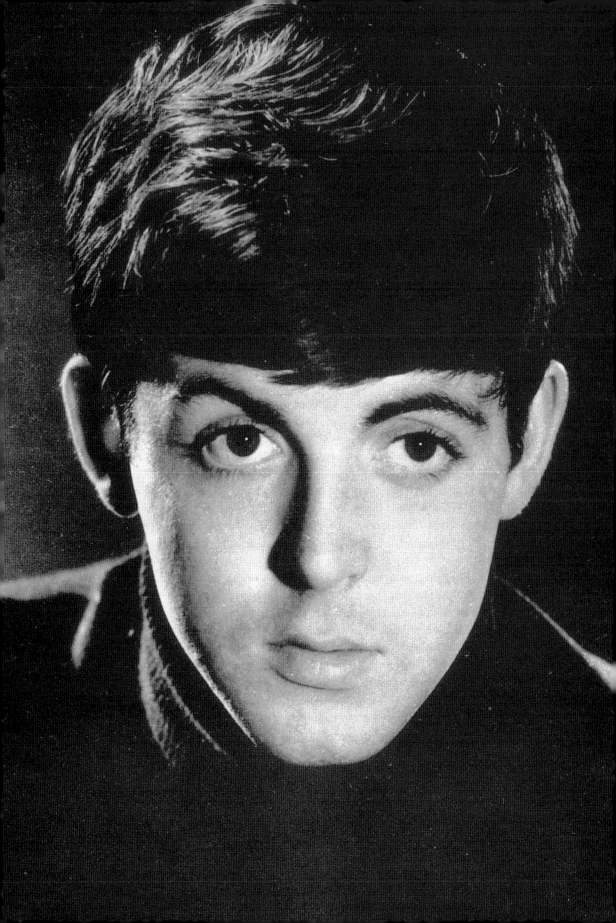

drumming beatle . . .

Ringo Starr

By just three months RINGO beats John Lennon into the position of eldest member of The Beatles. He didn't join the group until 1962 and came in to replace Pete Best. He'd played with a number of other Liverpool combos before that but, remarkably, he looks just about the most typical Beatle of the foursome!

At St Silas Primary School in Liverpool he was known as Dick Starkey; another infant in the same class, Ron Wycherley, has since become known as Billy Fury. Ringo moved on to Dingle Vale Secondary Modern School where he showed excellent promise at handicraft lessons, even if he didn't shine in things like mathematics and science.

From the very beginning, Ringo's talent has been built into his fingers. Today they throb with rhythmic action even when he's yards away from a drum-kit. Observing his prowess at creating delicately-fashioned objects in woodwork, his teachers suggested he should begin to play a musical instrument. Ringo wasn't impressed—until his parents made him a birthday gift of his first drum-kit and discovered that his true leaning was towards a particularly fierce style of percussive pounding! "Luckily," recalls Ringo, "they didn't object to my noisy practising sessions and, since I couldn't cart a flipping big set of drums to school, the teachers never had to put up with any play-time rehearsal sessions from me. But I did get into trouble for using my fingers as drumsticks on a classroom desk. Everyone else—including the teacher—was doing

some quiet reading and my constant rapping got o people's nerves. So they started rapping on me wi something larger than a drumstick but it didn break me of the habit".

Ringo had one very big dislike when he was school. He couldn't stand the soggy lunches the dished up. He remembers: "Several of us got to gether, pooled our money which was meant f school meals and went out to buy other thin instead. Mostly we shared a loaf, a few bags chips and five Woodbines!"

That fascinating "Ringo" nickname stems fro the vast collection of rings which adorn his bu fingers. Somebody once asked Ringo what sign ficance there was in the fact that he seemed to we the rings on a different hand each day. "Tha easy," he claimed, "they're far too heavy to ke on one hand all the time. I'd begin to walk with o shoulder lower than the other!"

When he left school Ringo couldn't decide b tween a career in hairdressing or motor racin Since he didn't have a driving licence the form might have been the obvious choice if drummi hadn't started to turn into a full-time occupation

Ringo thinks a lot but says very little until som one makes a point of involving him in conversatio His sense of humour tends to be of the poker-fac variety. His drumming produces one of the fine group-binding sounds in the business and he d clares that his first twelve months with The Beatl have been the happiest of his life to date.

RINGO'S BEATLETISTICS: Born in Liverpool, 7 July 1940. Measures 5 ft. 8 in., weighs 9 st. 8 lb. Eyes: blue. Hair: brow with grey streak over the right ear. Likes Ray Charles, steak with chips, fast cars, sleek suits and neatly-dressed gir Began with Liverpool's Darktown Skiffle outfit, drummed with other groups including Rory Storm's Hurricanes befo meeting The Beatles in a club and joining them in 1962. Dislikes travelling in the early morning, setting up his kit in hurry, onions, motor bikes and Chinese food. Has no brothers or sisters.

HE TLE BAC G C UND

in the black-and-white setting which inspired "Z Cars" and made "Maggie May" in
a music-hall joke.

BIG chimney stacks blowing clouds of darkening smoke into a low, grey sky. Tough but tiny tugboats burping out their messages of warning through a Mersey fog. Tall, once-white buildings blackened by the grime of an industrial jungle and still scarred by wartime bomb damage. Green corporation buses hauling a great city's workers through traffic-choked streets at rush hour. A pair of still-majestic Liver Birds looking out across dirty waters to the dry docks of Birkenhead and beyond. Lime Street no longer living up to the legends of "Maggie May's" hey-day but still arousing the curiosity of the new visitor with its austere ale houses and multitude of milk bars.

This is the colourless, joyless side of Liverpool, the sea-port city which was home to Tommy Handley and Frankie Vaughan and which (eventually) inspired "Z Cars". Servicemen remember Liverpool as an embarkation point. Punters know it as an address on a pools envelope. Everyone who has or has not visited Liverpool claims to know the colourless, joyless side of the city. But there is another side to this thriving place—the side where The Beatles were born and where their big beat was bred. Much of it is underground, as if the Liverpudlians wanted to escape from the darkness outside into the brightness below. The brightness of the big beat. The audio brightness which has made the walls of many a city basement bulge with young jivers since the earliest days of the skiffle boom.

There is the Iron Door Club where rock combos took over from traditional jazzmen in the early months of the 'sixties. There is the Cavern Club, renowned Palladium of the Mersey Beat circuit, where top groups draw capacity crowds at lunch-times as well as in the evenings.

The decor of these clubs blends in with the darkness of Liverpool's soot-stained public monuments. The brightness, the excitement, the gaiety, the thrills come from the performing groups and not from the dismal backdrops.

A single battery of white spotlights pierce through the smoke-filled, disinfected air to pick out the lean faces of the figures on the bandstand. Flashing guitars reflect thin rods of dazzling white light into the mass of gyrating stompers. Leather-clad youths pick out hefty metallic guitar phrases and cry thickly-accented lyrics from their stomachs.

This is the black-and-white background from which The Beatles emerged to captivate Britain pop pickers. This is where they learnt their uncompromising styles of singing and playing. This where the folk heritage of Liverpool music moulded itself into the Mersey Beat, a curious cross-breed Rhythm and Blues, Rock and Roll and sheer brute force soul-expression.

This is the side of a city which has made the word Liverpool mean something very important and something very new to millions of young people. Liverpool began to creep and then to scream in the music industry headlines towards the end last year as the birthplace of a monstrous new force which was destined to dominate the nation's hit parade by the middle of 1963. The force was led by The Beatles, undoubted monarchs of the Mersey Beat scene and now all-powerful invaders who threatened and then conquered much wider music continents in a series of determined thrusts and almost vicious onslaughts which were quite unprecedented in the annals of Tin Pan Alley history.

There is a high priest of Mersey Beat. His name is Bob Wooler. He knows every member of the city's more-than-a-hundred ultra-active combos. He's introduced each and every one of them to club and ballroom audiences all over Merseyside. He helped many to success by his backstage words of wisdom and his dressing-room discussions of encouragement and criticism. In December, 1960 was Bob Wooler who brought forward The Beatles to face their first suburban dance-hall audience. Of that début performance he used phrases like "musically authoritative", "physically magnetic" and "rhythmic revolutionaries".

Before the end-of-1960 launching of The Beatles founders John, Paul and George had spent the best part of the previous four years cultivating the instrumental and vocal policy, perfecting the highly individual style of presentation. At the same time they had been completing their education.

In the last years of the 'fifties John, Paul and George played at Chinatown strip-joints and church halls near Aintree race-course. In 1960 they trekked to Scotland at the request of Larry Parnes to accompany his latest Liverpool discovery—Johnny Gentle—on tour. They also toughened the texture of their voices and improved their instrumental technique by undertaking a strenuous season in Hamburg where groups are required to tear o

eir tonsils at seven-hour nighterie sessions. These
tal, formative years helped The Beatles to burst
to the Liverpool scene with an explosive new
und which soon moved them in from the suburban
ll of their début to the network of city-centre beat
sements.

News of their singular talent spread swiftly from
lar to cellar as The Beatles began to make fre-
ent appearances at the Iron Door Club and the
vern Club. Dozens of less experienced outfits
rted striving to drive the same type of power-
iven excitement into their music. But the pressure
uldn't be built up in time. The fact that they
led is underlined by the results of the 1961 popu-
ity poll conducted by the North-West's beat-
oup bible, *Mersey Beat*. The Beatles came out as
e year's clear favourites.

When The Beatles returned to Liverpool after
eir third trip to Hamburg in June 1962 a fantastic
Velcome Home" awaited them at the Cavern.
evious attendance records were splintered. There
s no longer sufficient room in the Cavern to hold
en a minor percentage of Merseyside's Beatle
ople. It was obvious that the group was on the
ink of something big. They were about to break
t of the Mersey Beat scene to reach a much larger
dience.

The man responsible for transferring The Beatles
m local to national and international fame was
ian Epstein, a superb manager with a far-sighted
siness brain.

Brian travelled up to London with tapes of The
atles and set their sounds before the ears of the
ght music business moguls. The big wheels of the
c industry stopped spinning momentarily, listened
and spun on indifferently. Revolutionaries are
dom accepted with any degree of immediate
diness.

In the office of E.M.I. recording manager George
artin, Brian discovered a wheel which was pre-
red to pause longer. Long enough to appreciate
t the contemporary hit parade could be knocked
sideways by the sound of The Beatles. Long enough
to accept a challenge and to gamble that The Beatles
would pack the type of shot-in-the-arm which the
1962 Top Twenty needed if it was to be saved from
virtual stagnation.

Injections are dangerous in big doses. The first
minor shot-in-the-arm was administered via "Love
Me Do", an October single issued through the
Parlophone label. The full-strength new Beatle
blood seeped through to 17th position in the charts.

Early in 1963 a second more severe dose stabbed
into the pop market. It was called "Please, Please
Me". It rushed to the very heart of Tin Pan Alley,
providing the Top Twenty with a timely stimulant
and The Beatles with something in the region of
half a million staunch new devotees from every
corner of the British Isles.

The reaction was swift and certain. The Beatles
were set up with a string of cross-country touring
dates. An L P album containing eight original Beatle
compositions went to the top of the microgroove
charts. The fabulous foursome collected Silver Disc
awards for "Please, Please Me" and their next
single, "From Me To You". An E P release head-
lined by John Lennon's dynamic performance of
"Twist And Shout" made record industry history
by selling faster than almost every contemporary
single. The Beatles culminated an initial year of
chart-smashing hits, bill-topping stage tours, fre-
quent broadcasts and spectacular television appearances by hitting the jackpot again with their fourth
single, "She Loves You".

There is no doubt that The Beatles will go down
as the dominating influence upon Britain's pop
music of 1963. What makes their achievements all
the more marvellous is the fact that each of their
chart-topping songs came (and will surely continue
to come) from the prolific pens of John Lennon and
Paul McCartney, the group's own built-in tunesmith team which puts some sort of extraordinary
pop magic into its infectious melodies and com-
pelling lyrics.

ENERAL BEATLETISTICS

sonal Management/Direction: Brian Epstein, Nems Enter-
rises Limited.

ording Manager: George Martin, E.M.I. Records Limited.

ord Label: Parlophone.

sic Publishing Company: Northern Songs Limited.

icial Beatles Fan Club: Anne Collingham (National
ecretary), 13 Monmouth Street, London, W.C.2.

icial Monthly Magazine: The Beatles Monthly Book,
44 Edgware Road, London, W.2

DISCOGRAPHY

Single play: Love Me Do/P.S I Love You. Please, Please
Me/Ask Me Why. From Me to You/Thank You Girl.
She Loves You/I'll Get You.

Extended play: Twist and Shout/A Taste of Honey/Do You
Want to Know a Secret/There's a Place.
From Me to You/Please, Please Me/Thank You Girl/Love
Me Do.
I Saw Her Standing There/Misery/Anna/Chains.

Long play: Baby It's You/Misery/Anna/Chains/Boys/Ask
Me Why/Please, Please Me/Love Me Do/P.S. I Love You/
I Saw Her Standing There/Do You Want to Know a
Secret/A Taste of Honey/There's a Place/Twist and Shout.

Beatling Beside the Seaside

You can't beat a nothing-to-do day beside the seaside. But you can Beatle it. Show-biz photographer Dezo Hoffmann had been looking forward to his summer day out of town. Nice quiet trip to the coast. Nice quiet day with The Beatles. Only the click of a camera to disturb the peace and calm of Dezo's day.

Quiet day with The Beatles? Never! Baring the unburnt body on a golden beach and letting the warm sun soak into every exposed inch of skin may be our idea of spending time beside the seaside. It

may be yours too. But The Beatles don't seem have a restful bone or a lifeless limb between the once they've caught sight of sea and sand. It's go, man, go!

With or without an attendant cameram there's nothing lazy or hazy about the days of su mer when George, Paul, Ringo and John get sniff of a brine-scented breeze! Lazy and hazy NO. Crazy ... YES. If you cast your eyes acro the next few pages you'll understand what mean ...

O KARTS GO! The thrills of the speedway track held hypnotic appeal for four eager Beatles. Cornering
seven miles an hour, man, that's something! If there was a boot for the guitars they'd swop their travelling
n for these nippy little jobs.

SOMEBODY TRYING TO MAKE AN ASS OF US? We counted five donkeys and four riders in this f[...] picture and we came to the conclusion that John was being greedy.

WHAT'S THIS? BEETLES FROM OUTER SPACE ATTACKING BEATLES FROM A BYGONE AGE? Someone must have sold this set of grandpa-type togs to the boys under the pretext that they're ideal for a British summer. The wind blows—they keep you warm ... the sun shines—they stop you getting too burnt. But we still don't know where those flying beetles came from although we guess there's an artistic young Fan Club member who recognizes her own handiwork!

Back Home with the BEATLES in their Booming BEATROPOLIS

So far as the current pop-business scene is co[n]cerned there's no denying that Merseyside h[as] become Britain's most booming beatropolis. He[re] The Beatles were born, here they cultivated the[ir] own brand of untamed beat music. There's a so[rt] of folk music heritage built around the basemen[ts] and ballrooms of Liverpool. It's a sort of rock a[nd] roll (but you'd tread on dangerous ground if y[ou] claimed it was out-and-out Rock and Roll). It's [a] sort of rhythm and blues (but you'd have the Chu[ck] Berry and Bo Diddley addicts jumping down yo[ur] throat if you called it pure Rhythm and Blues). It['s] a sort of Mersey Beat (but you mustn't refer to it [as] a Liverpool Sound because there's a world [of] difference between the vocal and instrumental styl[es] of the big beat city's leading combos). Let's ju[st] agree that most of the Merseyside groups produ[ce] sounds which are pretty fab—and that The Beatl[es] are the fabmost of them all.

The Beatles found their musical home in a seri[es] of subterranean cells beneath an all-but-dereli[ct] city warehouse. The cells are joined together by [a] coke bar, a stage, the minimum number of spo[t] lights and half a dozen black archways. The who[le] dim, musty, throbbing, thrilling, wonderful place [is] called The Cavern and it is the very heart of ever[y] thing the columnists have been describing as th[e] Liverpool Sound.

The Cavern has been like a musical mother t[o] The Beatles. Now the long-cherished offspring a[re] full-grown and have burst away from her ties. B[ut] the mother-and-son bond is still strong and Th[e] Beatles return to the Cavern whenever they ca[n] And, invariably, a mammoth welcome awai[ts] them ...

EARLY TRIUMPH FOR THE BEATLES. Presentation of an award made by the North-West's own publication Mersey Beat. *The Beatles topped that paper's annual popularity poll at the end of 1961 and 1962.*

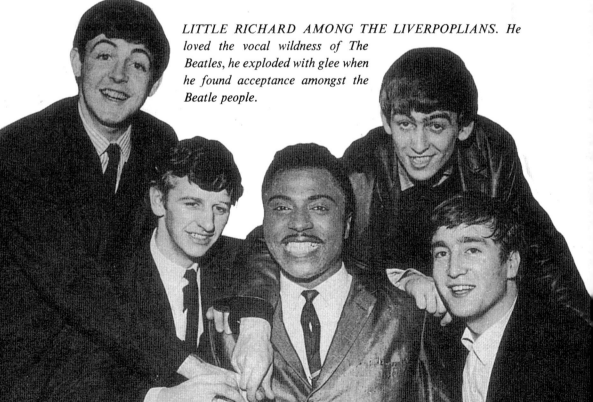

LITTLE RICHARD AMONG THE LIVERPOPLIANS. He loved the vocal wildness of The Beatles, he exploded with glee when he found acceptance amongst the Beatle people.

BUSINESS BRAIN BEHIND THE BEATLES

BRIAN EPSTEIN, 28-years-old director of the Liverpool management/direction firm of Nems Ent
prises Ltd., is the astute businessman behind the successful launching of The Beatles. A former R.A.D.
student, Brian first heard the boys in action at Liverpool's Cavern Club in October 1961. Customers of
city-centre record retailing stores operated by Nems had been asking Brian's staff for records by T
Beatles and the mounting local interest in the group persuaded Brian that he ought to take a look at t
foursome.

In December 1961 Brian signed The Beatles to an exclusive contract. Since then he has been responsi
for the personal management and direction of a number of other highly successful Merseysiders and t
star-stacked roster of recording artists now under contract to Nems Enterprises includes Gerry and T
Pacemakers, Billy J. Kramer with The Dakotas, solo singing star Tommy Quickly, dynamic Rhythm
Blues songstress Cilla Black and that brilliant bunch of off-beat singers and instrumentalists The Fourmo

By notching up a staggering advance order of over 300,000 copies for their fourth single, "She Loves You", THE BEATLES earned a Silver Disc Award even before the record reached the shops! BRIAN EPSTEIN (right) and E.M.I. producer GEORGE MARTIN (centre) help Paul, George and John to admire a precious Silver Disc trophy. Where's Ringo? We guess he must have been overwhelmed by the surprise presentation!

BRIAN EPSTEIN: A star-stacked roster of recording artists come under his personal management.

CHART-TOPPERS AT THEIR MOMENT OF TRUTH

the swift-spinning world of singles and L P's,
chart chances and silver discs, you're as huge or
tiny as your placing in this week's Top Fifty.
The days of reckoning come long before the release dates. They start in the early morning at the
recording studios. A publisher pops in to check last-
minute plans. Visitors are ushered away to hide
themselves in an upstairs control room. A dozen
red lights glow their warning and another moment
of truth arrives for the chart-topping Beatles. What
they sing and play within the next few hours will
decide their top-star value within the next few
months.
Will the freshly inscribed tapes carry the type of
pop material which is to notch up another half-
million jackpot winner? Up to six minutes of solid,
driving sound will eventually fill two sides of a Parlophone single. Six weeks of industrious work may
have gone into the perfecting of those six minutes
of sound. Six weeks from now The Beatles will
know if the quality of their next record release still
rates them Britain's Number One favourites with
the nation's pop pickers.

*FLASHBACK POSTSCRIPT ON THE SUBJECT
OF DISC-STUDIO SESSIONS: This very first
London photograph of The Beatles was taken when
they made their début decks—"Love Me Do" and
"P.S. I Love You" at E.M.I. in September '61.*

Stars of Stage, Home-Screen & Radio

MODERN methods of mass communication have helped to make the music industry move fast. A radio broadcast can help to build a hit record. A hit record can bring plenty of television exposure. Star status leads to bill-topping concert tours. Whichever way the teenager turns there is fresh pop music to be heard, bright new pop stars to be seen.

The Beatles have broadcast and televised many times during their first year in the business. They've starred in several cross-country stage tours, they've been made the central figures of a B. B. C. series called "Pop Go The Beatles" and they've been seen on the home-screens in the major musical showcases like "Thank Your Lucky Stars".

THANK YOUR LUCKY BEATLES. *These pictures were taken when The Beatles went to the A.B.C. television studios to show themselves to millions of viewers via "Thank Your Lucky Stars".*

EASY BEAT: The Beatles have drawn record listening audiences via their broadcasts on the Sunday morning Light Programme series. A rehearsal-break discussion involves George, producer Ron Belchier, Ringo and "Easy Beat" jazzman Kenny Ball.

POP GO THE BEATLES. Sandwiches and shirt-sleeves for a back-to-the-camera George while B.B.C. compere Lee Peters listens to Paul playing the harmonica. "Look! Only one hand!"

A London Day in the Life of the BEATLES

IT began as a free day in London—one of the rare and precious free days in the life of those busy Beatles. Nothing to do except a little shopping and a little looking-forward to the evening when the boys would receive their first Silver Disc award for selling far more than a quarter of a million copies of "Please, Please Me".

It began as a free day BUT …

9.30 a.m. Always somebody who needs a whole lot of coaxing before he'll get up in the morning. Paul's offer of a cuppa looks as though it might produce positive results with an idle Beatle called John.

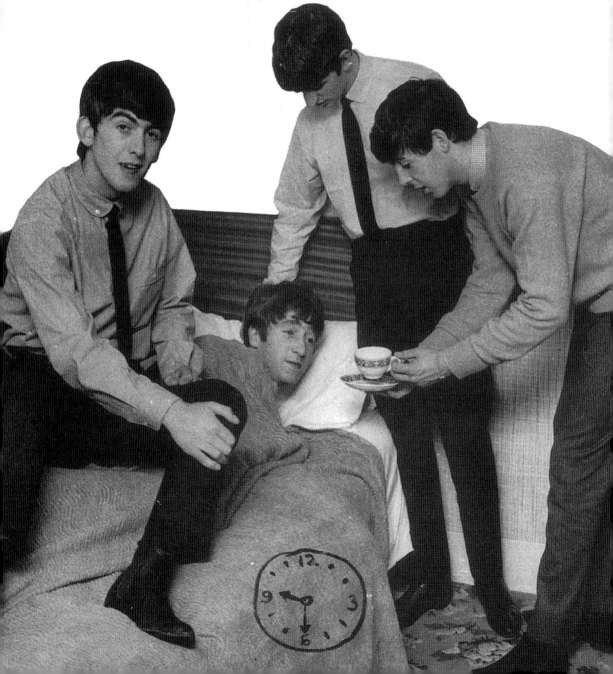

.00 a.m. Bedside breakfast in a London hotel room. Time to talk about yesterday's recording session and morrow evening's concert.

.30 a.m. Unscheduled visit from a glossy magazine's photographer delays The Beatles in the lobby of eir hotel. Willing porters help to provide an off-beat picture.

11.10 *a.m. Belated beginning to a Beatle-day. Boys set off down a peacefully deserted street of London W.C. They were due to arrive at their West End tailor's ten minutes ago!*

11.35 *a.m. Show-biz suit-stylist Douggie Milli makes special clothes for the top recording stars Britain and America. Today he was measur George for a new jacket—until Ringo chimed in w that smart wisecrack which triggered off a burst laughter all round!*

12.15 *p.m. Beatles buying bargains? The Italian shopkeeper thought he'd mastered the English language until the boys began to baffle him with their Liverpool slang. Paul speaks German and Spanish but that does really help.*

45 p.m. *Popsters posing in the park. A delighted young fan spotted the boys during her lunch hour and* *camera started clicking away in no time. Casual poses like this one seldom reach the newspapers.*

5 p.m. *Bob-a-bunch bananas for a light lunch? A side-street stallholder sells a few of his "very best* *cted".*

1.08 *p.m. Female fans materialize out of thin air wherever the boys go. These two blondes were only too happy to share Ringo's bag of fruit.*

1.35 *p.m. Bananas, strawberries ... and what will y have for dessert, sir? Two Beatles settle for cones soft ice cream and George likes to pretend he's g one too. Paul's either (a) not keen on soft ice crea or (b) keen on preserving his slim figure!*

2.00 *p.m. This silent Soho alley will be throbbing with activity after dark. Right now it provides the boys w a short-cut route to the photographic studios of Dezo Hoffmann.*

5 p.m. *Photographers who feed out new show-biz pictures to the press have to take every opportunity of replenishing their quickly consumed stockpile of Beatle shots. An hour in front of the cameras and spotlights provide another valuable selection of studio poses for Dezo Hoffmann.*

5 p.m. *More measuring—with the boys surrounded by sewing machines and shirt-fronts. Shirts take severe punishment during energetic stage shows—The Beatles change into fresh ones after every performance.*

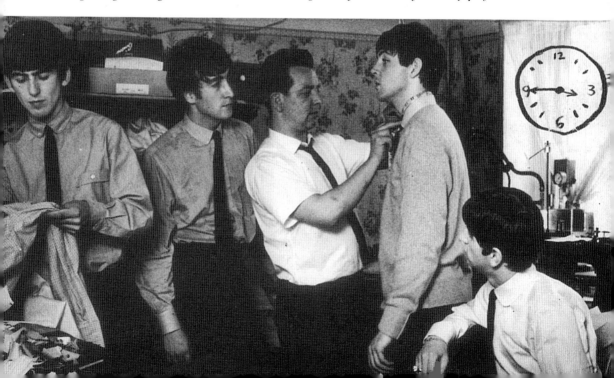

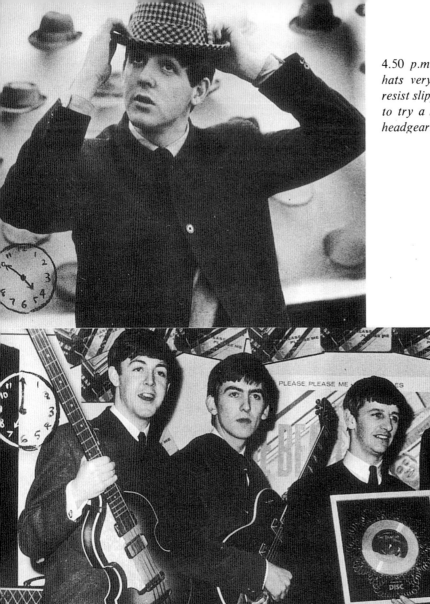

4.50 *p.m. The Beatles don't wear hats very often, but Paul couldn't resist slipping into a West End store to try a stylishly checked piece of headgear.*

7.00 *p.m. Culminating moment to the day's activities. Disc producer George Martin has just presented The Beatles with a "Please, Please Me" silver disc award. The auspicious ceremony is followed by a hectic press reception. Did we say this started out as a FREE DAY?*

11.00 *p.m. Back in Central London, and the hotel lobby. A late-night luggage check before the boys race off to the airport. They'll travel three hundred miles before dawn whilst road manager Neil Aspinall arranges for cases, clothing and instruments to be driven towards the next concert venue at the other end of Britain.*